Table of Contents

Chapter 1: Recognizing the voice of the Master

Scriptures: John 10:1-15 & Psalm 23

Key Verse: John 10:27

Growing up in the country, my family has always owned a dog. More accurately, we've always owned dogs, plural. I can't even think of a time in which we only had one dog at a time. Our dogs were family dogs, but for the most part they followed the commands issued by my mom. She was the one who cared for them, so it was her voice that caused their ears to perk up and their tails to wag.

My husband, Taylor, and I have four dogs of our own, and the same behavior occurs in our little pack. I feed them, bathe them, care for them when they are sick, and as a result, they listen and respond to me much more eagerly than they respond to him. And strangers won't get any cooperation from my dogs. They don't care if you get mad when they refuse to cooperate, and they aren't concerned with trying to please you. They don't know you, they don't trust you, and furthermore, they don't care if you get frustrated when they ignore you.

My dogs know my voice. They know the tones of my voice and what those tones mean. You might be able to trick them by using something that smells like me, by mimicking the whistle pattern I use to call them, or by driving up in my car about the time I should be arriving home from work, but you can't fool them when it comes to my voice. They know the voice of their master.

Humans tend to think of themselves as the superior species, but as I was reading through the tenth chapter of John one day, something struck me. Like dogs, many types of livestock also become attuned to the voice of their caregiver, be it a shepherd, farmer, or rancher. The animal knows that voice, trusts that voice, and follows that voice without fear. As Christians, do we know the voice of our Master?

This world is a noisy place, and there are many distractions. Can we successfully pick out our Master's voice from among the noise? Recognizing His voice requires that we spend time with Him. My dogs are with me nearly every day of the year, and because of that, they know my voice. If they heard me only once a month – or worse only on Christmas and Easter – they wouldn't know my voice. They wouldn't follow me, and I couldn't keep them safe and healthy.

As Christians, we must be able to recognize the voice of our Master, and that only comes from spending time with Him. Prayer, Bible reading, and church attendance are some of the ways we can develop regular habits of spending time with God. He is the Good Shepherd, and John 10:27 tells us, *"My sheep listen to my voice; I know them, and they follow me."* When we spend time with God, we learn to not just hear His voice, but to listen to it. For His part as our caregiver, He knows exactly how to best meet our needs, because He knows us like no one else ever will. He will meet all our needs, if we will just follow Him.

In the 23 Psalm, David described the Lord as our Shepherd who leads us to green pastures and still waters. Notice that He doesn't "drive" us or "herd" us, He "leads," which means that following Him is a choice. There are consequences if we choose not to follow Him, and usually, those consequences are unpleasant.

If dogs, sheep and other livestock can learn to distinguish and respond to the voice of their master, I certainly don't want to be so "superior" that I fail to realize my own need for a Master whose voice I can trust.

I love my dogs and want what's best for them, but how much more does my Heavenly Father love me and want what's best for me? Well, He loves me enough to lay down His life for me – and you too – because He is the Good Shepherd. Let's learn to listen to the Master's voice, and follow wherever He leads.

Prayer: God, give me the desire to spend more time with You, and come to know You better as my Shepherd. I know You want to care for me and protect me, and I know there is no one else better prepared to do that than You, my Creator. I want to learn to recognize and follow Your voice, because I trust you to lead me through the difficult times as well as the times of rest and refreshing.

Chapter 2: Staying in the Master's presence

Scriptures: Psalm 27:1-10

Key Verse: Psalm 27:4

Of the four dogs in our pack, Scruff is the one who consistently stays closest to my side. Wherever I go, you can count on her being just a few steps behind me. And because of this, I've accidentally shut her in the closet on more than one occasion.

Aside from being my permanent shadow, Scruff also spends a lot of time looking at me. When she does occasionally allow some distance between us, she makes sure to position herself so she can see me at all times. If I move, she moves. It doesn't matter if I'm moving from the couch to the recliner, going to grab something from the bedroom, or – heaven forbid – stepping into the bathroom and expecting a little privacy, she's coming along too, even if it means sitting outside the bathroom door while I take a shower.

I've become so accustomed to her presence that I hardly notice her behavior anymore. I think about it when my nephews giggle at her, or when my husband shakes his head at her dedication, or when I trip over her and get frustrated that she's under my feet.

I was having one of those days a few weeks ago when I tripped over her for about the fifth time while trying to clean house. I could feel my frustration level rising, and I whispered a quick prayer under my breath. One of those short, spur-of-the-moment prayers I find myself praying more and more. It went something like, "Lord, give me patience for this little dog that loves me." I turned on some music and continued with my work. Before I knew it, God was working on me while I was working on the floors.

It wasn't long before I was back to appreciating the unconditional way Scruff loves me, yet what God was revealing to me through my little dog was this: what would my life be like if I was a little more like Scruff? More specifically, what if I wanted to be in God's presence as much and as often as Scruff wanted to be in my presence – what would that look like?

You see, Scruff doesn't really want anything *from* me; she just wants to be *with* me. She wants to be with me all the time, in any location, and under any condition. As long as she's with me, she doesn't care about anything or anyone else – she's content just to sit near me. Reflecting on that reality, I realized this little mutt was giving me a perfect example of what my devotion to God should look like. I also realized...I have work to do.

In Psalm 27, David gives a beautiful description of the Lord. He is one who is our salvation in times of fear and danger, and one who will never abandon us, even though we may be betrayed by those who are closest to us. As I reflected on what had just been revealed to me, it was verse four that stood out, *"One thing I ask from the Lord, this only do I seek: that I may dwell in the house of the Lord all the days of my life, to gaze on the beauty of the Lord and to seek Him in His temple."*

Just to be in His presence. That is enough for me. Why? Because I know that all the other cares of this world fade away when I'm in His presence. I never have to leave His side because He is capable of being in all places at all times, but I do have to desire to be near Him. Being in His presence will mean saying no to things that will draw me away from Him. It will mean saying no to things that take up precious time I could be spending with Him. But if my greatest desire is to sit near Him and look upon the One who loves me, those will be easy choices to make.

I want to live a life devoted to God, and I'm thankful for a little furry mutt that reminds me what that looks like.

Prayer: You are everywhere at all times, Lord, and yet You desire to spend time with me. Help me to be more aware of Your presence throughout my day, because I know You are always near. Give me the strength to turn away from the things that will pull me away from You, and grant me the wisdom to make choices that keep You as the first priority in my life.

Chapter 3: Curiosity

Scriptures: Acts 17:16-34

Key Verse: 1 Timothy 6:20-21

Dogs are a bit like people in that they seem to be born with certain personality traits. Ozzie, my golden-eyed Shar Pei mix, was born with a curious nature that knows few boundaries. Oz is also a very intelligent dog, and when you mix intelligence with curiosity, sometimes the results are quite funny.

For example, if one of the other dogs has something Ozzie wants, he will literally stage a scene to divert their attention. Usually, he pretends to see a squirrel or goes running to meet a fake someone pulling into the drive. He carries on the charade just long enough to circle back around to the now abandoned item, snatch it up, and carry it off. This routine happens on a regular basis.

On another occasion, he carried home a neighbor's chicken. Thankfully the bird was alive and unharmed, but I was more than a little shocked to open the door and find him basking in the sun with a new chicken friend sitting calmly beside him. He'd never seen a chicken before, and I suppose his curiosity won out.

From getting his head stuck in a few tights spots to being covered in soot from the burn pile, and from thoroughly inspecting a new toy to being a first class escape artist, we get plenty of laughs from this dingy dog. But his curiosity has also given us plenty of scares. He's been run over once, bitten by a snake four times, and kicked by a horse – and those are just the major incidents.

I love Ozzie's curious nature – I wouldn't change it for anything – but there have been times I wish he would have known when to stop. Had he stopped just a bit sooner, he would have saved himself from the pain, and he would have saved us the heartache of having to watch him be in pain.

I can't help but wonder if God feels the same way about us sometimes. I believe God created us to be curious. How else can you explain humans' insatiable nature for exploration and learning? We want to see new things, meet new people, go new places, and understand new concepts. God built that into us, and in His infinite wisdom, He designed a universe in which everything points back to Him.

This was exactly the line of reasoning Paul used to introduce the Gospel to the highly intelligent and curious Athenians in Acts 17:16-34. These people were curious, but in their search for God, they'd made false gods out of practically everything. They were worshipping the workmanship rather than the Workman who created it.

Curiosity is a God-given trait that helps us seek, find, and understand God, but as with most other traits, we must not let our curiosity run wild. If we do, it may take us down a path that leads to our injury. This was exactly what Paul explained to his friend, Timothy in the first letter that bears Timothy's name. Paul wrote, *"Timothy, guard what has been entrusted to your care. Turn away from godless chatter and opposing ideas of what is falsely called knowledge, which some have professed and in doing so have departed from the faith."*

This world offers many "truths," but rarely do these truths give us black and white answers. Instead, they add to the growing greyness that exists in our society, and often, they can cause us injury. Like Timothy, the truth of God's Word was entrusted to my care when I became a follower of Christ. Although society says there are many ways by which the curious seeker can find his god, the truth is that there is only one Way to the one God. (John 14:6)

For the purpose of finding common ground on which to start a conversation about the Gospel, it can be beneficial to have some knowledge of the other ways people seek to find God. However, I must not let my curious nature take me down any of the wide paths that lead to destruction. That goes for you too.

The fourth time Ozzie was bitten by a snake, he was bitten directly on the nose. I make note of this, because as I continue to explore the vastness of this universe, soaking up the knowledge God has to offer, I pray my curiosity will not lead me to stick my nose in places it doesn't belong, making me an easy target for that old serpent, Satan.

Prayer: God, I thank you for giving me a curious nature and for providing me with a complex world to explore. Help me to control that curiosity, and keep me safe from those who would lead me down paths of destruction. You have entrusted me with the Good News of Jesus Christ, and I ask you to help me guard that precious gift as I share it with others.

Chapter 4: Happiness

Scriptures: Matthew 5:1-12

Key Verse: Proverbs 16:20

We were still in college when we added a black lab mix to our family. A friend found the puppy abandoned alongside a highway in Tahlequah, Oklahoma, and somehow I talked Taylor into keeping him. I wanted to spell his name, "Beau," but Taylor said we weren't fancy enough for that, so "Bo" it was.

From the start, Bo was a completely different dog than Ozzie, who was about six months old at the time. Bo was mellow, not mischievous, and the little guy was always happy. Even when being scolded, his tail would still be wagging.

Nine years later, Bo's personality is much the same – the dog is always happy. He's happy when we get home, happy to play with his toys, and happy to meet new people. He's happy when riding in the car, happy when he's swimming in the pond, and happy when lying in a pile of leaves.

We call Bo the million-dollar dog, because despite his happy-go-lucky personality, the dog has managed to rack up the vet bills over the years. But even when recovering from some of the painful surgeries he's had to endure, Bo always seems happy. His tail never ceases to wag.

I know a lot of people who are like this too. They face difficulties and hardships that most of us will never experience, and yet they never cease being happy. Death, persecution, hardship, and hunger – how do these people hold on to their happiness in spite of such grim circumstances? I believe the answer is simply this: they don't waste time focusing on their circumstances. They focus on the One who can bring good out of even the worst circumstances.

Matthew chapter five begins one of Jesus' most well-known sermons. It took place on a mountainside, and was aptly named, The Sermon on the Mount. In the first 12 verses of this chapter, Jesus introduces the crowd to eight statements that we now call the Beatitudes. Even if they can't recite them by memory, many people have at least heard of the Beatitudes.

Several years ago I heard a sermon in which the pastor shared that one of the translations of the word "blessed" – which is used repeatedly in this passage – is "happy." I encourage you to try reading that passage, substituting the word "happy" where "blessed" is written. Upon first reading, you may still be confused. For example, how can someone who is persecuted (verse 10) be happy?

As humans, we want instant gratification. We want to be happy and we want it now. But Jesus' sermon did not put time limits or deadlines on our happiness. He simply promises that those who are persecuted, meek, mourning, etc. are happy. They are happy because they are not focusing on present circumstances. They are happy because they have placed their trust in the promises of God, and God always delivers exactly what He promises.

Proverbs 16:20 reads, *"Whoever gives heed to instruction prospers, and blessed is the one who trusts in the Lord."* The Bible is full of God's instructions for our life, and if we will follow those instructions we will prosper. This proverb goes on to say that blessed – or happy – is the one who trusts in the Lord. You and I can be happy in the highs and lows of this life if we put our trust in the God who never fails. He wants us to be happy.

As I write this, Bo is recovering from his second knee surgery. I am thankful for his happy nature during these past few weeks, because I truly think it has helped speed his healing. As a dog owner, it's difficult when I can't explain why I chose to subject him to such pain. Given his circumstances, this surgery was without a doubt the best choice, but it's still difficult to watch. I know Bo trusts me, and I am grateful for his trust, but I am even more grateful when he remains happy in spite of his circumstances.

By choosing to be happy regardless of my circumstances, I hope I can warm God's heart the way Bo continues to warm mine.

Prayer: Regardless of my circumstances, Lord, today I choose to be happy. I know that You are in control of every situation, and I know I can trust You in all things. I may not understand why I am facing difficulties, but I understand that You want me to be happy, so happy is what I choose to be.

Chapter 5: Courage

Scriptures: Deuteronomy 31:1-8

Key Verse: Psalm 27:14

Peyton is our smallest dog. For only weighing 35 pounds, this little terrier mix has an attitude that's more suitable to a German Shepherd. She's not the dominant dog of the pack – that's Ozzie – but I'm sure she's more than willing to take over if he ever decides to retire.

Living out in the country, there are plenty of things for Peyton to chase. It's comical to watch her chase something small like a squirrel because she gets a line down her back that makes her look like a tiny, hairy stegosaurus. At some point in the chase, Peyton realizes she isn't going to catch her prey. She stops abruptly, stares until the little creature runs out of sight, dramatically wipes her feet, and then trots rather smugly back to the house.

When it comes to squirrels, it's easy to be brave. She behaves a little differently if the animal is bigger. She still barks like the biggest dog in the yard, but I've noticed that if she's at all uncertain about what to do, she looks to me for direction. If I move forward, she's right there with me, albeit slightly behind me. If I retreat, so does she. Watching her behavior over the years has reminded me of how we should respond when we are scared, uncertain, or facing our own "big animal."

Some people might find the Old Testament boring, but I love reading through this rich history of God's people. The stories are vivid, realistic, and relatable, but sometimes we have to slow down and think about them in context. A perfect example of this can be found in Deuteronomy 31. After living in the wilderness for 40 years, the Israelites were preparing to cross into the land that God had promised to give them. They were going from being nomads in a desert wilderness to setting up permanent homes in a lush land full of natural resources. But there were two rather unnerving realities facing these people: 1.) Their leader was not going with them, and 2.) The land into which they were going was already occupied by some rather hostile nations.

The leader of the Israelites, Moses, was now 120 years old and nearing the end of his life. A man named Joshua had been appointed to lead the people onward. Knowing the Israelites would be nervous about marching into hostile territory without their trusted leader, God gave Moses a message for them. The whole exchange can be found in verses 1-8. Verse 6 is my favorite in that passage: *"Be strong and courageous. Do not be afraid or terrified of them, because the Lord your God goes with you."* This is a great verse to read whenever you're feeling afraid, but I'd like you to also pay attention to verse 3: *"The Lord your God himself will cross over **ahead** of you."* Think on that for a moment.

When we face a difficult situation, we can be strong and courageous because God is moving ahead of us. He is making a way for us if we will just follow Him. However, to follow God, we must wait on His timing. If we plunge ahead without Him, the results can be disastrous – there are plenty examples of this in Israel's history too. If we want to be victorious, we must wait on God to move first.

Psalm 27:14 advises us to, *"Wait for the Lord; be strong and take heart and wait for the Lord."* As you wait on Him to make the first move, pray about your situation. Ask others to pray with you. Read the scripture with an open heart, always listening for His promptings. Patiently waiting for His guidance can be difficult, but much less so than moving in the wrong direction and then dealing with the consequences.

Peyton has the good sense to wait for me before she plunges recklessly into the unknown. My presence gives her courage, and she trusts me to lead her to safety. When we are scared or uncertain, we can stand calmly behind the God who will lead us to safety, waiting on Him to make the first move.

Prayer: God, thank you for being my constant protector and shield. You are stronger and more powerful than any enemy I will face. I may find myself in scary situations, uncertain of what to do, but I know that You are with me. Help me learn how to wait on Your direction, and give me the courage to follow You wherever You may lead me.

Chapter 6: Washed Clean

Scriptures: Psalm 51

Key Verse: Isaiah 1:18

My dogs love to plunge headfirst into the slimy, murky waters of our pond. They don't even give it a second thought. Ozzie and Bo will stick their heads under water to troll around looking for frogs, while Peyton and Scruff come away wearing thigh-high boots made of mud.

One of the downsides to raising dogs in the county is all the organic material they can access. For those of you who dwell in the city, organic material is the polite way of saying rotting, putrid, maggot-encrusted animal carcasses. Be it a bird, an opossum, or the random body parts of a deer found during hunting season, my dogs love to roll in whatever pile of rank-smelling remains they can find. They also like to eat it, but that's a different story.

A dog's sense of smell is better than that of a human's, but I will never understand why they think death and decay equates to puppy perfume. What smells good to them does not smell good to me, thus there's no way I'm letting them in my house like that. No amount of self-grooming will get them up to my standards of cleanliness, and we have reached a standoff. They willingly take a dip in the cold, nasty pond, but when it comes to warm water and soapsuds, they run the other way.

My dogs hate taking a bath, and if I'm being honest, I don't much enjoy the bath routine either. It's hard work, it's messy, and it's the only time my dogs aren't looking at me with love.

Instead it's sadness, shame, and irritability I see in their eyes. But later that night, after everyone has dried off and mostly forgotten about the ordeal, all four pups sleep fantastically. They sleep well, because they are clean.

A warm shower is one of life's luxuries for which I am extremely thankful. It helps me relax, and I sleep better when I'm clean. We wouldn't think of allowing our physical bodies to wallow in filth, consistently refusing a good scrubbing, but too often that is the case when it comes to our spirituality. We look at things we shouldn't look at, say things we shouldn't say, do things we shouldn't do and all that sin adds up to a stinky spirit. But a shower won't wash off this stench. In fact, the only thing we can do is turn to the One who can give us the spiritual cleansing we need.

Most people think of King David as a hero – someone to be admired. This is true, but he was also a human who made mistakes. His biggest mistake was secretly sleeping with another man's wife and then having that man killed. Yep, King David was an adulterer and murderer. But the truth always has a way of floating to the surface. David's actions were found out, and God in His mercy forgave David of his sins. Why? Because David truly repented. There are less than 20 verses in Psalm 51, but you can easily see the agony David felt over disappointing his God.

In Psalm 51:7, David asks God to wash him, making him whiter than snow. David's request mirrors language found in Isaiah 1:18 where the Lord is speaking to His people who have continuously rebelled against Him. After describing the sad state into which their disobedience has led them, God gives them hope in verse 18: *"'Come now, let us settle this matter,' says the Lord. 'Though your sins are like scarlet, they shall be as white as snow; though they are red as crimson, they shall be like wool.'"* God's promises do not expire. If we will come to God just as we are, sin-stained and ready for a change, He will wash us clean.

I don't give my dogs a choice when it comes to their own cleanliness. I imagine that God would prefer we not get dirty, because the cleansing process may not be an enjoyable one for Him or us. Yet in His love for us, God gives us the free will to make our own choice, and He stands ready to wash us when we come to Him for cleansing.

Prayer: God, I realize that I live in a sinful world. Sometimes I find that the day's interactions have left me dirty without my choosing, and sometimes I actively participate in wallowing in the mud. Help me to see the dirt spots and come to You for cleansing before the stains set. Yet even when the stains are deep, I know You can make all things new.

Chapter 7: Worry

Scriptures: Matthew 6:25-34

Key Verse: Philippians 4:6-7

I don't know if dogs can actually worry about things or not, but if they can, Scruff is definitely the worrier of my pack. Unlike the other three, she can't seem to relax. The other three will be snoring loudly, belly up in their beds, and poor little Scruff is curled up with one eye open.

Scruff has been in our family for nearly a decade now, but when we first met her, she was a tiny pup abandoned alongside a lonely country road in the middle of winter. There were multiple puppies in the group, and we'd found several of them the day before we spotted Scruff. She and another little one had spent a scary, cold night all by themselves. Thankfully, Scuff and her littermates' story had a happy ending. Still though, I can't help but wonder if that experience had a lasting impact on her.

As a child, worrying wasn't part of our life. We didn't worry, because we were too busy enjoying life. Our responsibilities were few, our world was small, and many of us were lucky enough to have adults who shielded us from scary things. Now that we're adults, things have changed. We worry for ourselves, for friends, for loved ones, for the groups and individuals we see on the nightly news – we worry a lot. But why do we worry? Here's my theory: we worry because we aren't in control.

I am an admitted control freak – just ask my friends and family. I always have a plan, I expect things to operate according to plan, and if I have to deviate from the plan, I worry. What if this happens? What if so-and-so doesn't like it? What if it costs too much? What if...what if...what if....so much anxiety from two tiny words.

In all His goodness, God is breaking me of this worrying habit. There's nothing good or healthy about worrying, and it doesn't do anything to bolster my faith. I wish I could tell you I was cured overnight, but the truth is it's day-by-day. It's a mental battle to choose NOT to worry, but thankfully, I am armed with something sharper than any two-edged sword. I have the Word of God.

Whenever I feel worried thoughts beginning to assault my mind, I turn to Matthew 6:25-34. In my Bible, these words are in red, which means Jesus is speaking them to His listeners. In this passage, Jesus reminds me that God knows and will meet all my needs. All I need to do is walk outside and look around – He cares for the birds and the flowers of His creation, and He loves me more than those, so He will care for me too.

For added effect, He throws a rhetorical question in verse 27, *"Can any of you by worrying add a single hour to your life?"* A rhetorical question is one that doesn't need an answer because the answer is already obvious. In this case I think it's both rhetorical and ironic because worrying will actually take hours from your life.

In my daily battle against worry, I also find it helpful to speak scriptures out loud, and my go-to verse is Philippians 4:6-7 which reads, *"Do not be anxious about anything, but in every situation, by prayer and petition with thanksgiving, present your requests to God. And the peace of God which transcends all understanding will guard your hearts and minds in Christ Jesus."*

Instead of worrying, ask for God's help. Thank Him for supplying your needs, even when you don't yet have an answer, and have faith that He will take care of it. If this is the attitude you adopt, an otherworldly peace will flood your heart and mind. People watching your situation will wonder how you are so peaceful in the midst of a storm.

Scruff sleeps most deeply when I let her sneak into bed with me. She tucks herself tightly into my side, and with my arm around her, she's softly snoring within minutes. Turn your worries over to God, and then settle in for the best night's sleep you've had in a long time.

Prayer: Worrying solves nothing, Lord, and yet I find myself worrying about things, people and situations outside my control. I know You are the Master of the universe, nothing is too hard for You, and nothing surprises You. Teach me to turn to You instead of wasting time with worry, because You are the only One who can give me peace in the midst of life's storms.

Chapter 8: Freedom

Scriptures: 1 Corinthians 10:23-33

Key Verse: Galatians 5:13

Ozzie has always been an escape artist of the finest quality. I will never forget when I came home to my apartment in college to find this tiny pup sitting in the middle of my living room next to a pile of... well you get the picture. The baby gate was still up across the entryway to the kitchen, so I was puzzled as to how he got out. I plopped him down on the other side of the gate and watched the replay.

Although not much bigger than my hand, this problem-solving pooch wedged himself into the tight space between the trashcan and the gate and then wriggled himself up and over the gate. For those of you who watch American Ninja Warrior, imagine a dog doing the Jumping Spider obstacle. This was the first of many great escapes.

Living out in the country, Ozzie enjoys his freedom. He likes to roam the nearby woods and honestly, I don't worry too much about him. He's a savvy dog that stays clear of the roads and keeps a good distance from strangers. I like it that Ozzie enjoys his freedom to the fullest, but I don't like it when our other dogs do the same. The other three are not as intelligent as Oz – they get in the road, wander too far in the woods, and they just don't have the same shrewdness that Oz displays. They aren't capable of handling the same level of freedom that Oz enjoys.

When it comes to Christianity, people tend to think there are a lot of rules that force Christians to live fenced-in lives. That perception is completely false. Really, it all boils down to only two: love God and love others. I find loving God to be a lot easier than loving other people, especially when those other people try to force me to follow their convictions. I am interested in living according to the Word of God, not according to the rules made up by people, Christian or not.

For example, I have found plenty of scriptures that speak against drinking to the point of intoxication. Christians should not become tipsy or drunk. Period. However, I have yet to find the scripture that forbids a person from enjoying a glass of wine over dinner. Despite this, there are Christians who maintain that drinking wine should be avoided because it is a sin. If they believe they should avoid wine, then they should avoid it for the sake of their own conscience, but they should stop short of expecting others to share this conviction. (For the record, I don't even like wine.)

But this coin has two sides. In our example, those Christians whose conscience allows them to enjoy a glass of wine with their dinner should be considerate of the people with whom they are dining. If a glass of wine will cause their dinner partner to be uncomfortable, start an argument, or worse end their relationship, the right thing to do is to skip the wine. By putting another person's feelings above your desires, you are displaying love toward your neighbor.

The extent to which we enjoy our Christian freedoms is exactly what Paul was speaking of in the tenth chapter of 1 Corinthians. Verses 23-33 give specific examples of how Christians are to enjoy their freedom while being sensitive to others, both believers and non-believers.

In another New Testament scripture, Galatians 5:13, we are told, *"You, my brothers and sisters, were called to be free. But do not use your freedom to indulge the flesh; rather serve one another humbly in love."* As Christians, we can enjoy a freedom the world will never understand, but we must always use that freedom for service, not selfishness.

Ozzie will continue to enjoy his freedom outside the fence, because he can do so safely. However, because my other three are incapable of safely enjoying that same level of freedom, I will be their gatekeeper. Christians must act as their own gatekeepers. While we enjoy great freedom, we must remember Paul's words that not all things are "beneficial."

Prayer: By studying the scripture, You make the truth clear to me, Lord, and it is by knowing this truth that I can live a life of freedom. Reveal Your truth to me, but as I learn, keep me from enjoying my freedom at the expense of others. Let me not forget that loving others is more important than the things that bring me pleasure.

Chapter 9: Fear

Scriptures: Romans 8:18-39

Key Verse: Isaiah 41:10 & John 14:27

Bo is our biggest dog tipping the scales at nearly 90 pounds. A majority of the time, he's also our most laid-back dog, the only exception being thunderstorms. One loud rumble is all it takes to reduce this big hulking dog into a whimpering, shivering scaredy-cat.

Once he's been thoroughly scared by a thunderous boom, the first thing Bo does is look for me. He searches franticly through the house until he finds me, and I spend some time petting him to calm him down. Within a few minutes he stops shaking, but he's glued to my side until the storm passes.

If the storm hits at night, I'm still on duty. I'll make him lie down on his bed next to mine, and if it's a really loud storm, I'll sleep with one arm hanging down so my hand can rest on his back. As I lay there trying to go to sleep, I can't help but smile at how much this guy trusts me. I can't do anything to quiet the storm, but as long as he knows I'm here, Bo will sleep soundly through the rest of the night.

As we change from children to adults, our fears change too. They change from monsters under the bed to fear of failure, financial ruin, or death. Social media and the news only add to our fears as we hear reports of terrorism, sickness, and planes disappearing from the skies. God never intended for us to live in fear, and I am convinced that fear is one of the weapons most frequently used by Satan. If he can keep us quivering in fear, then we won't be able to accomplish all God has planned.

When we think of the early church, most of us probably think of the great leaders like Paul, the miracles, and the thousands of people who were turning to Christianity. We forget these people were also enduring horrible persecution. Nero was the emperor at the time the Christian church was being established. If you didn't pay attention in history class, here's a quick recap: Nero was evil. The Christians refused to engage in the worship of the emperor as a god, and they refused to participate in the raunchy rituals required to worship many of the false gods prevalent in Rome. By taking this stand, Christians quickly became targets of persecution. Their punishments included everything from being fed to wild animals for the sake of entertainment, to being burned alive and beheaded.

This was the setting as Paul penned his letter to the Roman Christians. In the first half of chapter 8, Paul reminded his readers of the eternal life God had given them, encouraging them to behave like children of a King. In verses 18-30 he recaps the glorious future that awaits them after death. Finally, Paul closes the chapter by reciting an extensive list of things that, although frightening, can never separate Christians from God's love.

There are numerous scriptures that speak directly to fear: Psalm 118:6, John 14:27, 2 Timothy 1:7, Psalm 56:3, Joshua 1:9. When I am feeling afraid, I turn to one of these scriptures to reassure myself that all is well if I will just trust God.

One of my favorite verses about fear comes from Isaiah 41:10. God is speaking to the people of Israel who, facing terrible persecution, have scattered across the earth, fleeing from their enemies. He reminds them that He has chosen them for a special work and says, *"Do not fear, for I am with you; do not be dismayed, for I am your God. I will strengthen you and help you; I will uphold you with my righteous hand."* Regardless of what I face, God is with me. He will strengthen me, help me, and uphold me when I am too weak or scared to stand on my own.

Bo's fear of thunder dissolves when he feels my hand – my hand that can do nothing to calm the storm. What then do I have to fear when I can feel the hand of the One who can calm every storm?

Prayer: There are so many things in this world that stir up fear, Lord. But instead of focusing on those things, I choose to focus on You. Your hands hold me, protect me, and guide me through every circumstance. You never leave me, nothing can ever separate us, and regardless of the circumstances I face, I have nothing to fear.

Chapter 10: Greed

Scriptures: Luke 12:13-21

Key Verse: Ecclesiastes 5:10

Peyton eats like there is no tomorrow. The dog has never missed a meal, never gone hungry for a day while in my care, and yet she swallows most of her meals without chewing. I've tried multiple tactics to get her to calm down when eating, but nothing works. She may be the smallest dog of our pack, but she has the biggest appetite of the bunch.

It was a typical Saturday morning, which for the Thompsons means house cleaning. Chores come before fun, so Taylor and I were hustling around the house checking items off the chore list. I was cleaning out the refrigerator, and the dogs were licking their lips staring at the growing pile of leftovers that would soon be tossed into the yard. I made sure everything was safe for them to eat, herded them outside, and scattered the food across the grass.

Usually, I leave them to their grazing, but that day something made me stay. I stood on the porch, watching them search out and suck up each morsel, when I heard a funny noise from Peyton. The sequence went like this: funny noise, no noise, weird hunkering-down-with-strange-facial-expressions behavior. I began to panic as I realized she was choking. I yelled for Taylor and ran toward her, planning to pound on her back until Taylor could get there and administer the Heimlich.

Thank the good Lord, Peyton managed to dislodge the piece of chicken breast she'd been choking on. It was whole, of course, because she doesn't bother to chew. In that instant I went from being relieved to wanting to choke her myself. Her greed had nearly cost her life that morning, and I'm pretty sure she shaved a few years off my life as well.

From birth, humans seem hardwired for selfishness. Just watch a group of toddlers play and see which word you hear the most – I'm willing to bet it's, "mine." Selfishness and greed may come naturally, but God expects us to curb our sinful, selfish nature and become cheerful givers instead.

In Luke 12:13-21, Jesus tells a story of a rich farmer who was enjoying an abundance of crops beyond what he could use or store. Instead of looking for ways to bless others with his good fortune, the greedy farmer made plans to build bigger barns and keep all the crops for himself. This farmer wasn't judiciously planning for hard times; he was hoarding everything he could, not knowing he was going to die the very next day.

I once heard a bit of wisdom that says we should hold the blessings of God with an open hand. They are His to give and His to take. If we clench our fist tightly around them, it will hurt when He is forced to pry apart our fingers. And if our fist is clenched tightly around one blessing, our hand is not open to receive additional blessings. God gives, and because we should be imitating Him, we should be giving.

The author of Ecclesiastes is said to be Solomon, the son of King David. Solomon received a special gift of immense wisdom from God, and he was fabulously wealthy as well. The book of Ecclesiastes speaks extensively on the ways people foolishly waste their lives, and in Ecclesiastes 5:10, the wise and wealthy Solomon wrote, *"Whoever loves money never has enough; whoever loves wealth is never satisfied with their income. This too is meaningless."*

Society provides us plenty examples of this. Money by itself isn't evil. Money is an inanimate object incapable of harm or good unless used by humans. It's the act of desiring that money above all else that is evil. The same can be said of many other things: fame, status, power, etc. All of these things fade away, and none can go with us after death. Our greed hurts others, and although we may not realize it, it hurts us too.

As her master, I will make sure that Peyton's needs are always met. It frustrates me when she greedily doubts my goodness to her own detriment. I pray I will trust my Master enough to freely share the blessings He has given me.

Prayer: God, help me become a cheerful giver. Keep me from allowing greed to creep into my heart, and teach me to be a good steward with what You've given me. Remind me that the blessings You've given to me are not mine to keep – I am to use them in ways that will help others see Your love.

Chapter 11: Anger

Scriptures: James 4:1-17

Key Verse: Ephesians 4:26

It was close to 6 p.m. as I pulled into our driveway at the close of a typical workday. I traveled slowly up our long drive, mentally noting that we needed to mow. As I swung my car around to enter the garage next to Taylor's already parked car, I saw it – blood! Lots of blood. It was on the driveway, the floor of the garage, the wall, and spattered all over the white door leading into the house.

I slammed the car into park, turned it off and hurried into the house. There was a trail of blood along the tile leading from the garage to the kitchen, and at the end of that trail I found Taylor, Oz, and Bo, all sitting in the kitchen bleeding. Thankfully, no one was seriously injured, and Taylor, seeing the panic on my face, immediately launched into an explanation.

He beat me home by about 30 minutes, and saw Ozzie and Bo come running up to greet him as they always do. He stopped to get the mail, and as he pulled into the driveway, he noticed the two of them playing – or so he thought. As he got closer, he realized they were fighting! It took him by surprise because these dogs had been raised together, and never before this moment had they ever displayed any aggression toward each other.

He jumped out of the truck and went to break up the fight, only to find that neither dog would relent. In his attempts to grab their collars, Ozzie grabbed Taylor's hand by accident and crunched his index finger. When Taylor cried out in pain both dogs immediately stopped. Taylor's hand was bleeding, and the ears of both dogs were shredded and dripping with blood.

As I tended to wounds, I quizzed Taylor about what could have started the fiasco; he quite confidently declared that they had been fighting over a bone. A return to the scene of the crime confirmed his suspicion. Both dogs have plenty to eat, yet they ripped each other apart over a tiny, bleached out bone fragment.

Anger is a very natural response. Even God gets angry, and since we are made in His image, it should not surprise us that we experience anger. The main difference between God's anger and our anger is that His is rooted in righteousness, while ours is rooted in selfishness. We become angry when people do wrong to us, when someone is careless with our property, or when things seem unfair. If we were honest with ourselves, selfishness is the spark that causes our anger to ignite. This is exactly what James wrote about in the fourth chapter of the book that bears his name.

The Bible speaks to us frequently about controlling our anger because if we give free reign to it, anger can quickly become destructive. One verse in particular might surprise you because in it, God gives us the green light to get angry. That being said, however, He does not condone our sinning because of that anger. Ephesians 4:26 reads, *"In your anger, do not sin. Do not let the sun go down while you are still angry."* Paul penned these words, and I am so thankful God didn't tell him to write, "Do not get angry."

God knows I will experience anger – He made me that way – but He also expects me to develop the self-discipline necessary to refrain from sinning just because I'm angry. In addition, He instructs me to deal with my anger quickly, before the sun goes down, because it's not healthy to lose sleep by dwelling on whatever is making me angry.

That was the first and last fight Ozzie and Bo had. Their ears healed, as did Taylor's finger, but all three of them have scars. The dog's selfish desire for a bone erupted in a fit of anger that caused pain for each of them. Even worse, they caused pain for the person who loves and cares for them. Our anger can have the same results if we are not careful to control it.

Prayer: Lord, anger is an emotion You've created me to feel, but help me control the ways in which I express that anger. I don't want to hurt others, and I don't want to be known as someone who can't control her temper. Teach me to control my anger, to release it in healthy ways and if my anger has caused harm to others in the past, bring those instances to my memory so that I may seek forgiveness and reconciliation.

Chapter 12: Beauty

Scriptures: 1 Samuel 16:1-13

Key Verse: 1 Peter 3:3-4

The wiry-haired terrier mix looked quite different than her sleek-coated littermates. She already had the makings of a tiny little beard and lynx-like tufts of hair on her ears. We gave our friends and family their choice of these puppies we'd found alongside the road, but no one seemed interested in the one that was different.

We ended up keeping little Scruff – no other name would fit – and many years later, the funny looking pup that no one wanted is my constant companion. No one else may agree, but I think she's beautiful! A good deal of her beauty comes from her sweet nature. She's quiet, gentle, and obedient. She may not be an award-winning pure bred, but I wouldn't trade her for any of the dogs decorated in society's canine contests.

Standards of beauty are ever-changing. A quick look through the artwork of the ages and one can easily see how fickle we humans are when it comes to defining beauty. History aside, beauty also varies by culture. Scaring, tattooing, and lip stretching are all foreign to most Americans' idea of beauty, but these are popular beauty methods in other countries.

I recently came across a fascinating online article written by a lovely young reporter who sent an image of herself to photo editors in 25 different countries. She asked them to, "Make me look beautiful," and the results were quite interesting. Lip color, eye color, the shape of her face, skin tone…no two photos were the same. All were adjusted based on the standards of beauty applied in that country.

Living up to our society's definition of beauty isn't just a challenge for women – men feel the pressure too. Both genders are bombarded by advertisements and images of "perfect" bodies and faces. Let me be clear in that I believe God wants us to care about our appearance. We should practice good hygiene and maintain our health. The Bible is clear that we are to treat our bodies as the temple of God, but we must be careful not to focus solely on our physical appearance while ignoring what lies beneath the surface.

In 1 Samuel 16, God sends His prophet, Samuel, to anoint the second king of Israel. The first king of Israel had been everything the people wanted – tall and handsome. King Saul started off his reign on a good foot, but it wasn't long before he was disobeying God and heading down a disastrous path. In preparation for Saul's death, Samuel was to anoint Saul's successor, so he set out toward Bethlehem, looking for a man named Jesse. One of Jesse's son's would be the next king of Israel.

When Samuel arrives, seven sons of Jesse are paraded before him. As the first good-looking guy passed Samuel thought, "Surely this is the Lord's anointed," but God gently corrected Samuel's way of thinking by saying, *"People look at the outward appearance, but the Lord looks at the heart."* God wasn't seeking a king who would be beautiful in appearance only; He was seeking someone who possessed the heart needed in a good leader. Both would be found in a lad named David who was out tending to his sheep.

So how does God define beauty? We are told in 1 Peter 3:3-4: *"Your beauty should not come from outward adornment, such as elaborate hairstyles and wearing of gold jewelry, or fine clothes. Rather, it should be that of your inner self, the unfading beauty of a gentle and quiet spirit, which is of great worth in God's sight."* Unlike the world, God is unchanging. I would much rather be of great worth in His sight than to continually try to meet the world's ever-changing beauty standard.

I think Scruff is a beautiful dog, but I assure you she won't lose any sleep if you disagree. She knows that I love her just as she is, and the opinion of her master is the only one of any concern to her. May we be the same way when it comes to assessing our own beauty – caring only for the opinion of our Master.

Prayer: Father, thank you for making me beautiful. You created my unique outward appearance according to Your standards of beauty, and You continue to refine my inner beauty as You teach me Your ways. When the world tries to tell me how I should look or act, remind me where to turn for guidance: to You.

Chapter 13: Stubbornness

Scriptures: Numbers 14:20-45

Key Verse: Proverbs 29:1

Ozzie's stubborn streak has been present from birth. Although highly intelligent, he wants to do things *his* way. Sometimes his stubborn streak produces comical scenes, but other times, his stubbornness causes us both some discomfort.

When we were in college, Taylor had a small rental house with a glass front door. At night, the bugs would swarm under the light on the small front porch, some of them landing on the door. Ozzie was incessant at trying to attack the bugs through the door. Finally at my wits' end over scolding him, and concerned that he would break the door – I let him outside to have what he so badly wanted.

After a few snaps and misses, he finally crunched down on one juicy bug – a massive stinkbug! The gagging quickly ensued. He learned his lesson from this one, but I wish I could say the same thing about bones.

Living out in the country, the dogs are always finding something organic to munch on, and we refer to Ozzie as, "The Bone Collector." The dog always has a bone or fragment of a bone, and although we constantly take them away, he always finds another.

But dogs are supposed to chew on bones, right? Maybe, but Ozzie chews on too many bones. We've been to the emergency room once because he was full of bones, and I've lost count of how many times I've had to wrestle him down and dislodge a bone fragment stuck between his teeth or in the soft tissue of his mouth. Being a dog owner is dirty business sometimes, but it would sure be a lot easier if Oz wouldn't stubbornly persist in chomping on every bit of bone he finds.

Refusing to change our behavior or opinions in spite of the evidence – that's stubbornness in a nutshell. We know something is wrong or bad for us, but we like it. Or, maybe it's admitting that we were wrong that keeps us in our stubborn straits. Whatever the reason, stubbornness is not just a dog thing, it's a people thing, and as with all of the other human issues, God has something to say about stubbornness too.

The book of Numbers both fascinates and frustrates me. It's fascinating because of the creative, awe-inspiring ways God continually met the Israelites' needs. It's frustrating, because their stubbornness kept them from receiving the wonderful gifts God planned to give them.

In chapter 14, we find the Israelites rebelling against God's plan to lead them into the Promised Land. After all the miracles they've seen on their journey out of Egypt, they completely freaked out when their scouts report that giants are living in the land they are about to enter. They turned against God, their leader Moses, and the spies – Joshua and Caleb – who reminded them that nothing was too hard for God.

This stubborn refusal to trust God had become a pattern for these people, and God had enough. The Israelites didn't want to go into the Promised Land, so God would let them stay in the wilderness. Then they changed their minds again and decided to go into the Promised Land, even after God told them no. They tried it anyway, but without God fighting on their side, they were no match for the people inhabiting the land. Their stubbornness earned them a 40-year stay in the wilderness.

Proverbs 29:1 paints a clear picture of what happens to stubborn people. The scripture reads, *"Whoever remains stiff-necked after many rebukes will suddenly be destroyed without remedy."* Stiff-necked is a term used with farm animals such as oxen. If an animal was stiff-necked, it was stubborn and hard to control. A stubborn animal is of little use on a farm. When we refuse God's corrective rebukes, we too are of little use in accomplishing His plans.

I continue to scold and rebuke Ozzie when I catch him with a bone, because I love him, and I don't want his stubbornness to cause him harm. God corrects us because He loves us and wants to guide us toward blessings. If we stubbornly refuse his corrections, we will be destroyed by our own schemes.

Prayer: Lord, help me to be obedient to you instead of stiff-necked and stubborn. I know your plans for me are good, so help me to faithfully receive your guidance and correction. I trust you even when I can't understand your reasoning.

Chapter 14: Friendliness

Scriptures: 1 Peter 3:8-18

Key Verse: Luke 6:31

Within our four-dog pack, Bo is definitely the friendly one. Peyton and Scruff are shy around new people that visit our home, and Ozzie tries to act aloof. He'll come up for a quick sniff, but then he's off continuing whatever he was doing before the new person arrived. Not Bo though. He likes making new friends.

I should clarify that Bo is friendly only after we've given him the green light to accept the stranger's presence. We get a lot of uninvited guests, and part of Bo's job is to keep strangers outside the gate until we invite them in or turn them away. However, once we have called him off duty, he turns into a teddy bear ready to be best friends with whoever came to call.

Once on friendly terms with a guest, he's eager to usher them into his domain. He walks alongside them, puts his head under their hand to be petted, and if ignored for too long, he will paw the air to get their attention. Bo only has one bad habit when it comes to meeting new people: he sticks his head up ladies' skirts! I'm glad he's friendly, but that part is always embarrassing for both guest and dog owner.

Friendliness looks a little bit different among humans, but I think our goal in showing friendliness is similar to that of our canine companions. We want people to feel at ease and welcome in our presence, so we show ourselves friendly. A friendly countenance helps to disarm people, and it makes differences easier to accept. A good example is a language barrier. I am by no means fluent in Spanish, but the situation is much less stressful when the person I am speaking to is friendly in spite of the communication challenge.

Christians should be some of the friendliest people found in this world, but unfortunately, friendly is not the first adjective most folks think of when it comes to Christians. That's a sad state of affairs because I think friendliness is one of our most-effective tools for sharing the Gospel with others. The more I show myself to be a friendly person, the more people I'll attract into my presence. The more people I attract, the more opportunities I have to share the Good News: that God loved us so much He sent Jesus to save us from our sins.

In 1 Peter 3 verses 8-18, the apostle Peter wrote to believers about how they should behave on a daily basis. He reminds them to be loving and compassionate, repaying evil with good. Living a life so contrary to the worldly norm will no doubt cause others to pause and take notice, which is why we must be ready – verse 15 – to give a reason for why we act differently.

This sort of lifestyle described in detail by Peter can also be summed up by Luke, the writer of the New Testament book that bears his name. In Luke 6:31 he records a statement made by Jesus: *"Do to others as you would have them do to you."* Notice there is nothing conditional about this statement. It doesn't read, *"If they are nice to you first, do unto others..."* There are also no time limits mentioned here. There's no deadline or quota, because this is a lifestyle.

I like it when others are friendly to me, so based on the way I interpret this scripture, Jesus expects me to be friendly. There is no shortage of words you can suggest – forgiving, patient, fair etc. – when it comes to the way we want to be treated by others. If we want others to treat us in a certain way, we should begin by treating others as we'd like to be treated.

Bo doesn't consciously choose to be friendly – it's part of his personality. When facing a stranger, he depends on his master to tell him how to behave, and my commands change based on the conditions. My Master doesn't change, however, and neither does His command to treat others as I want to be treated. In this case, with friendliness.

Prayer: Father, help me to be a person who is friendly to others, even those I don't know. I want to be Your representative. Help me develop a lifestyle of friendliness so that people will notice I am different from the world and ask what it is that makes me different.

Chapter 15: Submission

Scriptures: Luke 1:26-38

Key Verse: James 4:7

If I were to give away an award for submission within my pack, it would have to go to Peyton. Next to belly rubs and treats, the thing she wants most in the world is to please me, so when I tell her to do something, she does it with little hesitation.

Unlike the other dogs, Peyton isn't just submissive when it comes to the things she likes to do, she's submissive when I ask her to do something she absolutely hates. She is by far the best behaved at bath time, she takes medication without a fight, and she is perfectly still when it comes to grooming procedures like brushing and nail clipping.

Among humans, submission is an unpopular and hotly debated topic. Though it's easier to submit to a loving, perfect God than to a flawed, selfish human, submission is still difficult to practice. It requires us to put aside our own desires and follow down the path that God wants to lead us. The really hard part about submission to God is when His path takes us in a completely different direction than what we had planned.

Besides Jesus himself, I can think of no better example of submission than Jesus' mother, Mary. Most every person is at least vaguely familiar with the Christmas story, but if you're like me, you probably rarely stop to consider how the people in the story might have been reacting to all that was going on. Both Matthew and Luke contain accounts of the birth of Christ, but I'd like to focus on Luke 1:26-38.

In this passage, the reader is introduced to Mary, a young woman engaged to be married. She is going about her daily routine, probably daydreaming a bit about what life will be like with her fiancé, Joseph, when all of a sudden something extraordinary happens. An angel appears. As if that's not life-changing enough, the angel delivers some rather shocking news to Mary: she is going to have a baby. But this isn't any baby; it's the long-awaited Messiah. Oh, and to add one more twist, she's going to have this baby without doing it the traditional way, meaning no sex.

Putting myself in her shoes there would have been tears – lots of tears – as I worried about what everyone would think of me. Would any of the people I loved – parents, siblings, friends – believe my fantastic story? With a scandalous pregnancy like this, I could forget about my dreams of happily-ever-after with my fiancé. I would have been angry that God disrupted my plans, but thankfully, the salvation of mankind did not depend on someone as selfish as me.

After hearing the news and asking a basic question – how is this possible – the gracious young woman responds: "'I am the Lord's servant,' Mary answered. 'May your word to me be fulfilled.'" In the very moment her world is turned upside down, Mary chose to submit to God's will. Even though it was impossible for her to understand all the implications, she trusted God enough to humbly accept His plan for her life.

Sometimes I wonder what would have happened if Mary had been unwilling to submit to God's plan. Going a step further, what would have happened if Jesus had refused to submit to God's plan and die in order to save mankind? Mary would likely have been lost to history and humankind lost for eternity.

James 4:7 reads, *"Submit yourselves, then, to God. Resist the devil and he will flee from you."* Satan tried repeatedly to kill an infant Jesus, and Satan played a dominant role in motivating men to nail Jesus to a cross. What he didn't know was that God was using obedient people to orchestrate a flawless master plan. If we will submit to God, He will use us to accomplish something that sends the devil running.

Peyton is willing to submit herself to a flawed and selfish master, and she's just a dog. My Master is perfect, so I have no excuse for refusing to submit. If I submit myself to God, my selfishness will flee right alongside the devil.

Prayer: Submission does not come easily to me God, but I know it is something I can learn to do. I trust Your plans for my life, that You want good things for me, so help me to submit to Your will even when I don't understand Your plans. I want to be a tool in the hands of the Master, but to be used by You, I must submit to You.

Chapter 16: Forgiveness

Scriptures: Colossians 3:1-14

Key Verse: Ephesians 4:32

Each of our dogs was abandoned as a puppy. It breaks my heart to think at some point in their life they were cold, scared, and hungry, unwanted by whomever it was that threw them out to die. I don't think they can remember that experience, and for that I'm glad. I'm thankful God used that experience to place them in my life, but if I could, I would have saved them from that trauma.

Unfortunately, there are a lot of dogs abandoned out where we live. My family and neighbors try to help them all, but some are too frightened from what they've experienced, and they won't accept our help. We manage to find homes for a lot of dumped dogs, and we keep quite a few too. It's not their fault some human chose to be irresponsible and inhumane, so instead of turning them away, we choose to show them compassion.

I won't say that dogs are capable of forgiveness, but by showing them kindness and meeting their needs, I do think we are able to help most of them forget about their past abuses. Yet even then, it takes years for them to fully forget. Months after being with us, they will still flinch at sudden movements, run from strangers, or eat like it's their last meal. They are not the same pitiful dog they were months before, but their past experience continues to influence their present behavior.

While often said in the same breath, forgiving and forgetting are two very different things. Forgiving is a conscious choice to overlook an offense committed against you. Forgetting is an involuntary lapse in the memory. When you forgive, you are not, by any means, downplaying or condoning the other person's bad behavior. You are choosing not to dwell on the offense and allow the negative feelings to imprison you.

Choosing to forgive does not mean that you forget the offense. I wish it did, because life would be so much easier if we could forget the really hurtful past experiences. Over time, the Lord has helped me forgive those who have wronged me, but the scars are still there, as are the memories. I do believe that God can help us forget, and that is a prayer I pray quite often: "God, you've helped me forgive, now help me forget."

Jesus himself talked repeatedly about forgiveness, and anything that our Lord mentioned more than once deserves particular attention. It was also a topic Paul frequently visited in his New Testament letters to the church. In the third chapter of Colossians, Paul talks about the different kind of life believers should live as followers of Christ. Forgiveness is one of the hallmarks of this new lifestyle. As Christians, we are to be kind, gentle, and patient, forgiving others just as God forgave us.

The message of forgiveness appears throughout the Bible, and one of my favorite verses on forgiveness is Ephesians 4:32: *"Be kind and compassionate to one another, forgiving each other, just as Christ in God forgave you."* I like this verse for a couple of reasons. First, it instructs me to be kind and compassionate. I am a lot more likely to forgive if I am focusing on trying to be kind and compassionate rather than vengeful and vindictive. Second, it reminds me that kindness and compassion are not enough – I must be kind, compassionate, AND forgiving.

But when I'm really struggling, it's the last part that gets me through. I am to forgive just as Christ forgave me. I didn't deserve to be forgiven, but He forgave me anyway, and at great personal cost. His painful death on a cross was for me – so I could be forgiven. If He could do that for me, then surely I can forgive others for Him.

My dogs lead a happy life. Their life is enviable for a number of reasons, one being that they live fully in the moment, not dwelling on the painful past. What comes naturally for them is a choice for me, but with God's help, I can choose to forgive and live freely in the present.

Prayer: Forgiveness is something you ask of me God, and yet it is a difficult thing to do. I need Your help. Help me to understand that forgiving people does not mean I condone what they did, just as Your forgiving me did not condone the sinful life I'd led. Help me to forget the pain of the past, and move forward in kindness and compassion.

Chapter 17: Keep Watch

Scriptures: Matthew 25:1-13

Key Verse: Matthew 24:42

Scruff is scared of practically everything. She's more likely to run away from danger than toward it, and any loud noise sends her diving for cover. I'm also not sure her eyesight is the best, and as a result she's skittish of even the people she knows until they are close enough for her to figure out that she knows them.

Despite all this, Scruff is a great watch dog – just not in the way you might expect. From the moment I leave her until I return, she spends the time watching for me. She's free to roam our large acreage with the other dogs, but she makes sure to lie where she can see our driveway. She listens for the specific sound of my car coming up the road or the squeak of the gate at the entrance to our drive, and she's even taken to sprinting home if someone says the phrase, "Mama's home."

I have to admit, it puts a big smile on my face to have this devoted little creature streak across the lawn to greet me. She may be one of the smaller dogs in the pack, but she outruns them all to get to me. Her reward is to be swept up into my arms and showered with affection. The other dogs eventually arrive and share in the greeting, but Scruff always seems to get the majority of my attention because she's always ready and waiting. If she wasn't, she might miss out on precious time with her master.

Like Scruff, we too will miss opportunities if we don't have a "ready and waiting" mentality. This is true personally, professionally, and spiritually. We never know what wonderful opportunity life might present, so we need to live our lives in such a way that we are ready to act when the time comes.

As Christians, we should also be living with one eye on the sky, watching for the return of our Savior. The Bible is clear that no one knows when Jesus will return to take His people to Heaven. It does, however, say there will be signs to indicate the time is drawing near. In Matthew 25, we are given advice on how to wisely prepare for His return.

In the first 13 verses of this chapter, Jesus tells a story of ten women - bridesmaids who are waiting to attend a wedding celebration. They did not know when the groom would arrive. Half of the women prepared for the unknown by bringing extra fuel for their lamps. The other half were lazy, assuming things would work out in their favor, and brought no additional fuel. The groom came during the night, and the ladies who were ready and waiting went to the celebration. The others missed the party all together, because they were unprepared. So it will be when Jesus returns. Those watching and waiting will join Him for an eternal celebration in Heaven.

This story is a parable, which means it has symbolic meaning. We are the bridesmaids and Jesus is the groom. I believe the oil represents the Holy Spirit. All who accept Christ are filled with the Holy Spirit, but sadly, some never tap into this resource. Too lazy to study, pray, and cultivate a deep relationship with God, they settle for just enough to get by, incorrectly assuming they can borrow from others.

In Matthew 24:42 Jesus tells the disciples, *"Keep watch, because you do not know on what day your Lord will come."* We are not told this so that we can live in fear, but so that we can live in hope. He died for our sins, went to prepare us a home, and gave us everything we need while we wait. We have the choice to watch and be prepared, or not.

The tedium of waiting and the joy of my arrival is a natural routine for Scruff but there's nothing routine about her joyful reaction. When my Master returns, I want Him to find me watching for Him. Ready and waiting, I want to bring a smile to His face when I jump into His arms.

Prayer: As I go about my daily activities, Lord, let me never forget that I am waiting for the return of Your Son. Help me to use my time and resources wisely. When Jesus comes for me, I want Him to find me busily going about His work, but with one eye expectantly on the sky.

Chapter 18: Perseverance

Scriptures: Romans 5:1-11

Key Verse: Galatians 6:9

Ozzie is a dog on a mission. He has an ongoing battle with the moles that tunnel through our property, and he has taken it upon himself to rid the world of as many of these dirt dwellers as possible. None of the other dogs are interested in helping him complete his mission, but that doesn't discourage Oz.

A few months ago, I was outside with the dogs and I noticed Oz was working on another "mole mission" by digging the largest hole I'd ever seen him dig. His entire top half was below ground level, and the dirt continued to fly. He would dig furiously for a minute or so in the rocky soil, then stop and lay down to rest while looking over his work. I watched this behavior for several minutes, but other than the hole getting bigger, nothing was happening.

I tried to distract him with something else, but he was not moving away from his work. Amused by his antics, I pulled out my cell phone to record a video, and that's when it happened. He caught it! The mole he'd been chasing through four feet of dirt, rocks, and roots finally squeaked his last. Although I felt a bit sorry for the mole – at least he died quickly – I was proud that Ozzie had stuck with it. He refused to be distracted or deterred by the hard work, and he was rewarded with success.

Every human on the planet has a mission to fulfill. It may take us a while to figure out what our mission is, but I am convinced that we each have something we are supposed to accomplish while we are alive. Figuring out the mission is the easy part, but completing it takes a lifetime of perseverance. We will face all sorts of obstacles and setbacks, and if we don't persevere in spite of the challenges, we will never experience the fulfillment that comes when we complete our mission.

History is full of people who became famous for their perseverance. Since the Bible is history, it should come as no surprise that its pages are also filled with examples of people who persevered. Paul is one of my favorites, and he received his mission while en route to Damascus. In Acts 9 a resurrected Jesus calls Paul to share the Gospel with Jews, kings, and Gentiles alike, but in accepting the mission, Paul could not have imagined all the obstacles he would face.

In the process of sharing the Gospel, Paul was arrested, beaten, stoned, shipwrecked, snake bit, and more. His life was full of hardships that came as a direct result of his mission, but he refused to give up. In fact, he rejoiced because of his problems. In Romans 5 Paul talks about how faith brings joy into a believer's life, and right there in verse three you can see that he's rejoicing over his problems. The problems teach him endurance, build his character, and enhance his expectation of the reward that awaits him once his mission is complete. Jesus went on to call *all* Christians to share in Paul's mission of spreading the Gospel.

Hundreds of years separate Paul and I, but knowing that he persevered through hardships I will never experience makes it easier to accept his advice. In Galatians 6:9 Paul wrote, *"Let us not become weary in doing good, for at the proper time we will reap a harvest if we do not give up."* The world is full of evil, and sometimes I get weary of doing good things – it seems like I'm outnumbered and my efforts make little impact. But I can't let my focus settle on my present work; instead, I must focus on my future reward.

For Ozzie, the thrill of eliminating another mole is all he needs to persevere through the rocks, roots, and dirt keeping him from his reward. Thankfully, the reward for which I am striving is not so temporary. My reward for completing my God-given mission is eternal life. So although I sometimes grow weary in doing good, I will persevere toward my reward.

Prayer: God, show me my purpose – the reason You placed me in this exact location at this time. I know each of Your children has a role to fulfill within the body of Christ, and I pray that You would help me accomplish that role to the best of my ability. When I am weary, give me strength to persevere and remind me that I seek a heavenly reward for a job well done.

Chapter 19: Seek Guidance

Scriptures: Joshua 9:1-14

Key Verse: Proverbs 3:5-6

The weather was perfect. Three of my four dogs were lounging on the deck when all of a sudden the peaceful scene erupted into complete chaos. Unaware of the pack of sleeping hounds, a tiny mouse had crept out onto the deck. It only took a few seconds for the first dog to catch the scent, and then there were dogs running everywhere.

Bo was napping in the sand below the deck, and the commotion startled him awake. He wasn't sure exactly what was going on, but the other dogs were after something, and he was missing out. He stuck his head around the corner at just about the same time the mouse came running at him. He still didn't have a clue what the other dogs were chasing, but there it was... at his feet... so he snatched it up!

After a few minutes, the dogs had settled back into their napping places, but I noticed Bo was acting strangely – he was nervously pacing around the yard. He finally came over and sat down in front of me, and I was surprised to see a tail hanging out of his mouth. I opened his jaws, expecting the little animal to fall to the ground, but to my surprise it jumped out and scurried off into the bushes!

I have no doubt that the other dogs would have quickly crunched the little animal, but it appeared that Bo had been taken so off guard, he didn't know what to do. Maybe he didn't know the mouse was edible. Maybe he wasn't hungry. Maybe he was just holding it because the other dogs wanted it.

Whatever was going on in his canine brain, he didn't know what to do next.

Sometimes life surprises us, and instead of seeking the Lord's guidance on what to do next, we just react. We spring into whatever action comes most naturally, because action makes us feel like we're making progress. If we don't take action, we may miss the opportunity, or worse, someone else may seize it before us. I was laughing at Bo's dilemma that day, but if I'm honest, sometimes I react and end up looking just as silly as he did with a tail hanging out of his mouth.

The life of Joshua provides us with examples of great courage, and it also offers us a glimpse of what can happen when we don't seek God's guidance before taking action. God told the Israelites to drive out all the evil people who were living in the Promised Land, and by the time the reader reaches Joshua 9, the people of Israel have won two major battles. But there was one group of people called the Gibeonites who resorted to deception instead of war.

With costumes, props and a well thought-out story, the Gibeonites tricked Joshua and the other leaders into signing a peace treaty. Joshua failed to seek God's counsel in the matter, and the result was a binding treaty that led to battle (Joshua 10) on behalf of the people who had tricked them (Joshua 9.) Thankfully, God is able to bring good from our mistakes, and He gave the Israelites another victory.

Whenever I am feeling impulsive or impatient, I've learned to stop and think on Proverbs 3:5-6, *"Trust in the Lord with all your heart and lean not on your own understanding; In all your ways submit to him and he will make your paths straight."* Whatever the situation might be, my understanding of it is vastly limited compared to God's, and I am foolish to push ahead without first seeking His guidance. I need God to guide my steps, because His way is the best way, even if it doesn't make any sense to me.

I wish I could say I am wise enough to always lean on His understanding, but that's just not the case. There are times I behave a lot like Bo when he caught the mouse. I rush ahead without seeking counsel and the results are neither what I expected nor wanted. In spite of my foolishness, my Master is always willing to help me out of my latest predicament – if I will just trust Him.

Prayer: Father, I need Your guidance in all aspects of my life. You know the past, present, and future, and I am foolish to proceed in decisions without first seeking Your guidance. In the hustle and bustle of today's world, teach me to pause and ask for Your wisdom before taking a step in any direction.

Chapter 20: Jealousy

Scriptures: Luke 15:11-32

Key Verse: Proverbs 14:30

Whether it's belly rubs, treats, or toys I strive for equity in my actions toward my dogs. Three of them are just fine with this practice, but Peyton wants all my attention all the time. She also wants all the treats and all the toys. She turns into a little green-eyed monster when one of the other dogs has something she wants, and she has earned the nickname, "Weasel," for the sneaky way she steals things from them.

Her jealous behavior manifests itself in a couple of ways, one of which has to do with the toys they share – she likes to eat them. Not play with them, mind you, EAT them. Peyton rarely plays with toys, but I am constantly taking toys away from her to prevent her from eating them. If I am using a toy to play with one of the other pups, Peyton will do everything possible to get it. If she succeeds, she will try to eat it as fast as she can so they can't have it back. Not only is this habit annoying, it's unhealthy. One toy lodged in her digestive tract is an expensive, painful vet visit from which Peyton might not return.

From a very young age we begin learning that jealousy is unacceptable. Despite this fact, it seems our self-centered society does everything possible to unravel our training. Jealousy can be present in toddlers, teens or thirty-somethings, but no matter what the age or the species, jealousy is never cute. Much of the Bible is God speaking to us through the prophets and apostles, but there are instances of

God speaking directly to us. The topic of jealousy provides us with one of those instances.

Many people forget that jealousy is listed among the Ten Commandments God gave to Moses. People are quick to remember, "Thou shalt not kill," but "Thou shalt not covet," doesn't usually jump to the forefront of our memory. I think part of that is because we don't use the King James word, "covet," too often, but I think the main reason is because we don't take jealousy as seriously as God does.

Not only did God take the time to write – in a block of stone no less – that we should not be jealous, Jesus also had something to say about jealousy. In the story of the Prodigal Son, most people focus on the behavior of the lost son who repented and came home to the open arms of his father. But as you read that story in Luke 15, take a moment to look at the behavior of the other son – the one who stayed home and followed the rules. He's far from happy over his brother's return and the party that's being planned for the occasion. His attitude can be summed up in one word: jealous. His father lovingly rebukes his attitude in much the same way I think Jesus would rebuke us. His father reminds him of the many blessings he has, and calls on him to be happy for his brother who has returned.

No matter our age or maturity level, keeping jealousy out of our lives requires on-going effort. When I feel that little twinge of jealousy over my friend's news of her vacation or pay increase, I must quickly capture that thought and turn it over to Jesus so the poison of jealousy doesn't spread within me. That remains true when it comes to complete strangers as well. Proverbs 14:30 reads, *"A heart at peace gives life to the body, but envy rots the bones."* The words paint an ugly but truthful picture: I can choose to live in peaceful contentment, or I can rot in jealousy.

61

Peyton can't understand my verbal warnings about jealousy. I could write it down, but she still won't comprehend. I can excuse Peyton's jealous, self-destructive behavior because of her ignorance. But when I can read God's warnings and hear when He speaks to me, I should not expect to be excused by Him. Jealousy is a sin that leads to rot, and I would much rather live healthy, happy, and content.

Prayer: Father, I know that in Your family, there is no place for jealousy. Your Word warns me against allowing jealous feelings to take root, but sometimes I struggle with these feelings. Remind me that You meet all my needs and provide many of my wants, and help me to enjoy the peace of a life lived in contentment.

Chapter 21: Gifts

Scriptures: 1 Corinthians 12:1-27 & Matthew 25:14-30

Key Verse: 1 Peter 4:10

Part of my nightly routine includes walking through the house and picking up all the toys. No, I don't have a houseful of messy children; I have a houseful of messy dogs. I can't blame anyone other than myself though, because I'm the one who buys the toys.

Each of my four dogs likes a different kind of toy. Bo likes things that squeak, Oz likes things that crunch, Peyton likes soft toys, and Scruff likes ropes, but Ozzie and Bo get the most excited with a new toy. Although they are both long past the puppy stage, both turn into frisky little pups when I hand them a new toy. And I must confess, I get so much joy out of watching them play with their new toy that I want to give them new toys all the time, regardless of the fact that they will lay scattered through the house until I pick them up.

Gift giving – it's something we humans enjoy doing, but because we are born selfish, gift giving is a behavior that must be learned. Parents enjoy giving gifts to their children, because they find joy in watching their child play. Children also learn to give and experience the joy that comes from gift giving, and the cycle continues to the next generation. Gift giving is indeed a learned behavior, but it should come as no surprise that we enjoy it – we are made in the image of a God who also enjoys giving gifts to His children.

Like any earthly parent, God only gives His children good gifts. No parent would purposefully choose to give his or her child something dirty, broken, or harmful, and the same is true of God. Likewise, human parents know their children and what they most desire. God also knows His children, and He has no limitations in giving them what they desire most. Despite these similarities, there are two key differences in God's gifts versus those given by earthly parents.

First, God's gifts are often not as tangible as a child's request for a bicycle or video game. In 1 Corinthians 12, Paul spends the first 11 verses outlining the nine spiritual gifts God gives to Christians. The list includes intangible gifts like faith and prophecy, but it also includes things like healing and miracles, both of which can be seen and experienced by the senses. Paul then moves on to paint a picture of how these gifts are to be used within the body of Christ. Every member of the body has a role to fulfill, and if the member cannot fulfill that role, the whole body suffers.

Second, while gifts from our earthly parents are typically intended for our sole use and enjoyment, the gifts God gives us are intended to be shared. God gives spiritual gifts, but he also gives talents like athleticism, artistic ability, musicality, etc. He did not give us these gifts so we could selfishly hoard them for ourselves like the "wicked, lazy servant" described in Matthew 25:26, He expects us to use them for His glory.

I Peter 4:10 reads, *"Each of you should use whatever gift you have received to serve others, as faithful stewards of God's grace in its various forms."* Notice that Peter says we have each received a gift. No one is left out when God distributes gifts, but for reasons that only God understands, some people receive more gifts than others. Through prayer and self-reflection, we can discover what gifts we have received and how God wants us to use those gifts. We can even ask for additional gifts, and if our motives are right, God will grant our requests.

Once we discover our gift or talent, the next step is to begin using it. What parent wouldn't be disappointed if his child set aside his gift and never used it? I am disappointed when I purchase a toy that my dogs don't like because it sits wasted and unused in the toy box. I think the same is true of God. He takes great pleasure in giving us gifts, but it delights Him even more when we use those gifts as He intended.

Prayer: God, I know You have created me with specific gifts that are to be used to enlarge Your kingdom. Help me to recognize those gifts and have the courage to use them as You lead me. Teach me to appreciate the gifts I see in others, and show me how we are to work together as the body of Christ.

Chapter 22: Self-Confidence

Scriptures: Psalm 139:1-24

Key Verse: Colossians 3:23

Every so often a siren or the whine of a low-flying plane will set off an impromptu puppy serenade. Peyton is usually the first one to sound off, followed by Bo and then Oz if he's around. A few seconds into their song, listeners will hear these odd high-pitched squeaky yelps. That's Scruff. Try as she might, the poor little dog cannot howl.

Already smiling at how silly they all sound, I can't help but admire Scruff just a little bit more than the others. She doesn't come close to sounding as good as the other dogs, but that doesn't stop her. She's right there in the middle of her pack contributing as best she can. Sometimes the other dogs pause to look at her, but she doesn't know that her attempt at howling is just plain awful. Regardless of their stares, she closes her eyes, throws her head back, and squeaks out her part of the song.

If we find ourselves in a situation where our abilities and talents are not quite on the same level as the people around us, most of us will shrink back from whatever the activity might be. One reason for this behavior is that people are... well, judgmental! We see the stares, hear the whispers, and cringe at the laughter aimed in our direction. A second reason we hold back is that we compare ourselves to others. We judge ourselves not to be on the same level as those around us, so we decide it's better to sit it out rather than risk embarrassment. Both of these reasons will keep us on the sidelines of life unless we choose to think differently.

66

The Bible has a lot to say about judgment. In Matthew 7:1-3 and Luke 6:37-42, the authors advise us to stop judging and criticizing others or else we will be judged and criticized. The greater measure by which we dole out judgment, the more judgment we will receive. When it comes to judging others, it's clear that we should refrain from it, but what about passing judgment on ourselves?

God has given each person spiritual gifts and talents to be used. We're naturally good at some things, we have to practice at others, and then there are some things we will never be able to do well no matter how much we try. Regardless of our own self-consciousness and how others might rate our abilities, Psalm 139:14 gives us a boost of self-confidence: we are wonderfully made. Throughout this Psalm, the author reiterates that God knows everything about us, and we are precious to Him. He leads us, and He has a plan for us.

Scripture is clear that we are to hold ourselves to certain standards, and examine our motives for doing something, but we must be careful not to judge ourselves into a state of inaction. The Bible is full of examples in which people were asked to give their best effort and then sit back and watch God work: the fall of Jericho, Gideon's army, the widow of Zarapeth, and David's defeat of Goliath. God took their best efforts and worked miracles.

One of my very favorite Bible verses is Colossians 3:23, *"Whatever you do, work at it with all your heart as working for the Lord, not for human masters."* I like this verse because it reminds me that I'm not giving my best effort in the hopes of pleasing people; I'm giving my best effort because that's what pleases God. In those moments when I'm feeling less than confident in my abilities, I remind myself that God isn't demanding perfection. He's just asking for my very best effort at whatever it is I'm doing.

I'm not perfect, and sometimes my best effort, much like Scruff's howling, earns me the stares of others who are wondering if that's really what I meant to do. However, the God who can make anything out of nothing is asking me to give Him my best effort, not a perfect performance. When I do, He'll more than make up for my shortcomings, and when God works, people stare in awe.

Prayer: God, help me focus less on pleasing others, and more on pleasing You. I want to give You my best effort in everything I do, and where I fall short, I believe You will help my shortcomings. Teach me to be confident in the abilities You've given me, and always remind me that all glory belongs to You.

Chapter 23: Gentleness

Scriptures: Galatians 5:16-26

Key Verse: Philippians 4:5

I often joke that I'd like to train my dogs to help with the house cleaning, but so far the only task they've seemed to master is helping me clean out the refrigerator. When they see me headed outside with a stack of plastic bowls just removed from the fridge, they go from calm to crazy in a matter of seconds.

No longer dogs, I'm now surrounded by three snapping alligators, all hungrily eyeballing whatever morsel I might be holding. I've been nipped on more than one occasion if my release was too slow, so my approach now is to toss the leftovers into the yard rather than risk losing a finger. The exception to all of this madness is Ozzie.

He may crunch squirrels, moles, and rabbits with reckless abandon, but when it comes to human contact, he's a perfect gentleman who delicately takes whatever it is you're offering. He's also gentle with little kids and puppies. When he's had his fill of their antics, he will simply wander off rather than getting grouchy. Neither age nor illness affect his gentle nature, and because of this, I have no qualms about allowing him to approach people. I know he won't cause them harm, because he is gentle.

As Christians, we should display this same sort of gentle nature that puts people at ease when approaching us. Now enjoying the benefits of the salvation Christ gave us, our job is to help other people be reconciled to Christ. If we claim to be

Christians but are cranky, harsh and quarrelsome, why would anyone want what we claim to have, let alone have the courage to approach us to find out more?

But gentleness doesn't come easy for everyone. We live in a world that teaches us that gentleness is equivalent to weakness, and if only the strong survive, we cannot afford to be weak. However, like most things the world promotes, this is in exact opposition to what God tells us. While it's true that we have a hard time being gentle on our own, God gives us a powerful resource to help produce a gentle nature within us.

In Galatians 5:16-26, Paul writes to the early church offering advice on how to become the Christ-like people they so long to be. Like us, these Christians became new creations the moment they accepted Christ as their Savior, but they still had much to learn in their daily walk. Old habits are hard to break, and most of the habits we develop from years of worldly living need to be broken. These habits, behaviors, and ways of thinking don't change overnight, but by the daily process of allowing the Holy Spirit to guide us, we begin to produce things that are not of this world: love, joy, peace, patience, kindness, goodness, gentleness, faithfulness, and self-control. These are known as the Fruit of the Spirit, and they are only produced when we allow the Master Gardener to cultivate our heart and mind.

There are many days when I just don't feel like being gentle. My patience is depleted, I don't feel well, I'm irritated – the list of excuses goes on. It's those days I think on Philippians 4:5, *"Let your gentleness be evident to all. The Lord is near."* For me, this verse is a good reminder that the world is watching. Will they see someone who responds with gentleness? Will my gentle response set them on a path toward finding a relationship with Christ? Will my response please the Lord, who remains constantly by my side not to spy on me, but to give me the strength I need to live according to His call?

Ozzie's reward for his gentle nature is a lion's share of the treats being handed out. He has also earned my complete trust when interacting with people, and he's the dog I am most quick to introduce to guests. As I continue to allow gentleness to be produced in me, my Master also offers me blessings, as well as opportunities to meet new people and lead them gently to Him.

Prayer: Father, teach me to be gentle. Keep me from responding to others out of frustration or impatience. When people look at me, let them see Your love in my words and actions, and use me to reach those who are lost and hurting.

Chapter 24: Acceptance

Scriptures: John 8:1-11

Key Verse: Luke 6:37

I've lost count of the number of dogs that have been abandoned near our house. While we can't keep every dog that people heartlessly discard, we always give them what help we can, even acting as a foster home. But keeping a dog for any length of time usually results in some inconveniences for those in my household.

Ozzie hates it when we take on a new dog for any length of time. He shows his displeasure by avoiding us and the new dog for several days if not weeks. Peyton and Scruff pout – they glare and growl at the new dog and refuse to be anything remotely close to tolerant.

Bo is the shining exception. Having a new dog around the house for a few days doesn't bother him. Although a bit stand-offish at introductions, he's the first to accept and play with the new dog, and he only gets cranky when the four-legged stranger gets too close to his food bowl. Taking his cues from us, he accepts the new addition to the pack and goes on with his carefree life without missing a beat.

In some ways, people are more like dogs than they want to admit. When it comes to accepting those of our own species, sometimes we can be more prone to snap and snarl than warmly welcome a newcomer. We can be especially unfriendly when we've fallen into the trap of judging – and let's be honest, we're all guilty of passing judgment on another person at one time or another.

We judge them based on what we know of their past, their family or their actions. We judge them based on hearsay, what we think we know. We judge them based on our own emotional state, the feelings we have about them in the present or have felt about them in the past. Have you noticed yet how self-centered we are when we judge someone? We're judging them for our own benefit – to make ourselves feel better or justified – not because our judgment helps them in some way.

In John 8, verses one through eleven, a group of religious leaders attempted to trap Jesus with a question about judgment. They bring to him a woman who had been caught in adultery. I've often wondered why she was the only person called out for this crime that obviously involves two people, but this fact just supports the argument that human judgment is flawed. The religious leaders were prepared to kill the woman as the law directed, but Jesus, who brought us mercy and forgiveness, stopped them with a simple, wise comment that soon had them scattering.

Be sure to catch the last thing Jesus says to the woman in verse eleven. This is important because He was not turning a blind eye to her sin. He was not condoning her sinful act. He tells her very straightforwardly to leave her life of sin, but notice that He does not judge her. Jesus lived a perfect life and had every right to pass judgment on people, yet He serves as our example to leave the judgment to God. We can often see when a person leads a sinful lifestyle, and we are wise not to become their close associate; however, we must stop short of acting as their judge.

In Luke 6:37 Jesus spoke these words: *"Do not judge, and you will not be judged. Do not condemn, and you will not be condemned. Forgive, and you will be forgiven."* I believe this

73

applies to our relationship with both God and man. In both cases, we can expect to receive the same measure of judgment, condemnation, and forgiveness we dole out. It's that simple.

I will meet his needs even with an extra dog in the house, so Bo is accepting of other dogs. I will be fair in handing out rewards or punishments, my love for him will not diminish, so he can be secure in just enjoying life. My Master wants to save every lost soul that approaches, and my role in His household is to simply accept them as they are.

Prayer: Never let me forget, Lord, that I have no right to judge others. You are the fair and righteous Judge. You chose to forgive me, so how can I justify holding a grudge against others? Help me to display love and acceptance toward every wayward soul who seeks to find the One who paid the penalty for their sins.

Chapter 25: Persistence

Scriptures: Luke 18:1-8

Key Verse: Luke 11:9

Oz may be my most stubborn dog, but Peyton is by far the most persistent. This is true of many things, but especially when she thinks food is involved. Any time I step out the back door, she is convinced I've thrown food out into the yard. As I continue going about my business, not responding to her desire to go outside, she begins the persistent process by staring at me. That progresses to pacing, scratching at the door, whining, and eventually a bark or two if I continue to ignore her.

Eventually her persistence wins out, and I finally open the door, but this only happens after I've weighed many other factors. Is the weather suitable for her to be out? Is there anything in the yard that might hurt her? If there is food, is it safe for her to eat? She is oblivious to these things, but as her master, they are things I must consider.

Though I often shake my head at her antics, I have to give Peyton due credit for her persistence. The other dogs will give up and move on to other pursuits if I don't quickly respond to their petitions, but not her. She will persistently keep at it until she gets what she wants.

Persistence is a trait that is all too uncommon in today's culture. We like things to be quickly and easily acquired. Opposition to our aims and delays in our plans are frustrating, especially when these obstacles stand between us and the enjoyable things we desire. Yet in most cases, if we are persistent, our efforts will be rewarded.

But how much more frustrating is it when we must be persistent in pursuing those things which we deeply desire? Things like unanswered prayers, lifelong dreams, or miscarried justice. The need to be persistent is not new to mankind, nor are the feelings of frustration and hopelessness that can sometimes arise while being persistent. In fact, the need for persistence was a topic of conversation for Jesus and His disciples.

In the beginning of Luke 18 we find the story of the persistent widow. In the account, we hear of a widow who repeatedly pleads her case before a corrupt judge. The judge finally gives her the justice she seeks, not because it is the right thing to do, but because she persisted in seeking justice. Jesus concludes by pointing out that if an evil judge will eventually give in to persistence, how much more quickly will our just God hear and answer our persistent prayers?

I do not know why God expects us to be persistent. Perhaps He uses the time between petition and answer to change us – to help us see what it is we should really be seeking. Maybe the persistence on our part leads to a greater appreciation when the prayer is answered. Or, could it be that God is answering our prayers in an even bigger way than we could ever imagine? One that might take a little longer than we'd planned? Whatever His reason, we can take comfort in knowing that while He expects us to be persistent, He also gives us a wonderful promise.

In Luke 11:9 Jesus said to the disciples, *"Ask and it will be given to you; seek and you will find; knock and the door will be opened to you."* Each of these commands requires action on our part, and as in real life, I think sometimes we have to be persistent in asking, seeking, and knocking.

Before you use this as your opportunity to pray for a lucky lotto ticket, I encourage you to read the verse in context. Jesus is teaching the disciples how to pray, which includes praying according to God's will and Word. We must not make the mistake of pursuing our desires over God's plan for our life.

Peyton's persistence in seeking an open door is always rewarded, but often not according to her timetable. The door opens at my discretion – when conditions are safe and in her best interest. We serve a just, righteous God who sees our persistence, promises to respond, and rewards us at just the right time.

Prayer: Father, Your Word tells us that if we ask, it will be given. Teach me to ask according to Your will and not my own selfish desires. Remind me to be persistent when Your answer is delayed, and strengthen my faith so that I can learn to trust Your perfect timing.

Chapter 26: Friendship

Scriptures: Ecclesiastes 4:9-12

Key Verse: Proverbs 18:24

Peyton and Scruff are always together. Although they look quite different, they are sisters from the same litter of puppies. They sleep together, play together, eat together, travel together, visit the vet together– nearly all of their life experiences have been shared.

If ever scared or uncertain about what to do, these two stick close together. They protect and comfort each other, and although they were raised alongside Ozzie and Bo, Scruff and Peyton have a much stronger bond. Where Ozzie and Bo are comfortable by themselves, Scruff and Peyton are inseparable companions.

Yet despite their close bond, they do have their occasional fights. Their fights never escalate to the carnage of Ozzie and Bo's epic battle. They don't fight over food or toys or attention – their fights are more of an, "I'm sick of looking at you and need my space," type of spat.

Family and friends are an important part of our lives no matter what our age. They offer us stability, reassurance, and acceptance, and our life is enriched because of their presence. Well, it can be an enriching experience, if we choose our friends wisely. We have no choice when it comes to selecting our family, and we all have those family members we love – as well as those we love to avoid. When it comes to our friends, however, we are given the opportunity to be selective.

The book of Proverbs has quite a lot to say about friendship:

- Friends should be selected carefully – *"Make no friendship with a man given to anger, nor go with a wrathful man lest you learn his ways and entangle yourself in a snare."* Proverbs 22:24-25
- Friends love one another despite flaws – *"A friend loves at all times,"* Proverbs 17:17
- Friends tell the truth, even when it hurts – *"Wounds from a friend can be trusted, but an enemy multiplies kisses."* Proverbs 27:6
- Friends forgive – *"Whoever would foster love covers over an offense, but whoever repeats the matter separates close friends."* Proverbs 17:9

Beyond Proverbs, one of the best Biblical examples of friendship is that of David and Jonathan. Their story is found in the second half of 1 Samuel. Despite the complicated dynamics of their situation – Jonathan's dad was trying to kill David – their friendship remained strong. These men encouraged one another, told the truth even when it hurt, and protected each other at great personal risk.

Ecclesiastes 4:9-12 offers a beautiful description of our need for friendship by listing several reasons why two are better than one. When working with someone we receive a double return on our work, we have someone to help us when we fall, and we have someone to keep us warm when the world turns cold. Just like a rope is stronger when there are multiple strands woven together, so are we stronger when we choose to interweave our lives with those of carefully selected friends.

Proverbs 18:24 reads, *"One who has unreliable friends soon comes to ruin, but there is a friend who sticks closer than a brother."* There are those friends in life when once found, will be closer to us than our own flesh and blood. But I see a double meaning in this verse. In reality, my friends can't be with me at all times, they can't offer me supernatural protection nor do they know how to fix to the trials I face. But God does, and He desires to be my friend. Jesus proved that when He died for me, His friend. (John 15:13)

When I see the connection between Peyton and Scruff, I am reminded that family and friends are an important part of my life too. As their master, I am glad to see their strong bond, but I also desire a strong bond with each of them individually. I think God has much the same desire for us. He wants us to have earthly friends and He gives us advice on how to wisely select those individuals, but He also wants to be our friend. Although it is said that dog is man's best friend, in reality it is God who is man's best friend.

Prayer: God, I thank You for the friends in my life. I thank You for the wisdom and comfort they share with me, and I thank You for the many memories we share. Help me to be wise in selecting my friends now, and in the future, and lead me to people who will strengthen my walk with You.

Chapter 27: Warts and All

Scriptures: John 4:1-30

Key Verse: Romans 5:8

A few years ago I noticed something odd on the side of Ozzie's face. As it turns out, my sweet-faced little pup had managed to grow a nasty looking wart on the side of his head, near his eye. It's smaller than the tip of my pinkie finger, but it's still gross.

Every so often, Oz will come back from one of his jaunts through the woods with blood running down his face. He's fine, but the wart is missing. The first time it happened I was somewhat thankful, glad to be rid of the alien invader, but it grew back. Despite many more times of being ripped off his face, it always reappears.

Ozzie might not win any beauty contests, and other people might draw back in disgust when then see it, but the wart didn't change my behavior toward Oz, nor did it change his behavior toward me. We both know it's there, but its ugliness does not change our relationship. Sadly, when it comes to warts, things often don't go as smoothly in our human relationships. People judge us based on our appearance, and no one has a high opinion of warts.

A wart is just a small rough growth on the skin, but I think we can also have warts that are invisible to the eye – rough experiences or poor decisions that leave negative things growing just beneath skin surface. Maybe it's a bad divorce that left bitterness growing within you. Perhaps it's a traumatic childhood that left you with an inability to trust. Or maybe there's a secret sin in your life you can't seem to eliminate. Like a physical wart, it's roots stretch deep beneath the surface, and no matter how many times you tear it off, it comes right back.

People's reaction to our warts can cause us to avoid relationships all together, but that's not what I want to focus on in this chapter. I want to focus on how our warts can prevent us from having a relationship with God. In John 4 we find Jesus and his disciples traveling through a region called Samaria. The disciples went into town to find food, leaving Jesus sitting all alone near a well. Before too long, a woman of the city came out to fetch water, and Jesus asked her for a drink.

Without going into a lengthy history lesson here, you should know that the Jews and Samaritans did not get along at all, so it is surprising to the woman that Jesus, a Jew, would speak to her, a Samaritan, and ask for her assistance. As their conversation continues, we learn that the woman has been married five times, and the man she's currently living with is not her husband. After revealing His identity and marveling her with His wisdom, the woman forgot what she had come to do. She also forgot all about her invisible warts that caused others to recoil. Instead she ran back into town to bring everyone out to meet Jesus, the Messiah.

The disciples were surprised at this exchange between Jesus and the Samaritan woman, but that's because they were viewing the scene through human eyes. Human eyes have a hard time seeing past the warts. When Jesus looked at the woman, He loved her – warts and all.

Romans 5:8 reads, *"God demonstrates His own love for us in this: While we were still sinners, Christ died for us."* God doesn't expect us to get our act together before we approach Him, He wants us to come to Him just as we are. We have nothing to be ashamed of because He is our Father who loves us – warts and all.

Often Ozzie's wart is the first thing people notice about him, and while I can see it too, it's really very nearly invisible to me. I am an imperfect human, and yet I can see past the unattractiveness of Ozzie's wart and love him just as fully as when I first saw him. In spite of my warts, how much more does my perfect, righteous Creator love me? More than I will ever understand.

Prayer: In spite of all my flaws, God, You loved me enough to send Your Son to die for me. You never give up on me even when I make mistakes, and though I am far from perfect, I am Your cherished child. When the enemy calls attention to my imperfections, let me hear Your loving whispers that remind me of just how much I am loved by the Father.

Chapter 28: Rest

Scriptures: Genesis 2 & Luke 10:38-42

Key Verse: Matthew 11:28-30

If resting were an Olympic event, Bo would be the undisputed champion. He gets a full eight hours of sleep every night and it's a feet-up-in-the-air, deep snoring kind of sleep. He naps several times a day, laying in the yard, eyes half open soaking up the sun, and when I do convince him to have a bit of exercise with me, he's sure to rest up once we finish.

Before you label him as lazy, you should know he does a marvelous job of chasing away small animals and protecting us from strangers who wander up. He does whatever task I ask of him, but between tasks, you can be sure that he's resting up, and avoiding anything that might cause extra stress.

Unlike Bo, I don't have the luxury of spending part of every day napping in the sun. In fact, I don't rest well at all. I'm a doer. I like to be up and about, doing things that make me feel productive, and if I'm not careful, I can get carried away in whittling down my to-do list and completely ignore God's command to rest. That's right, God tells us to take time to rest.

A day of rest is mentioned for the first time in Genesis 2:3 when God Himself rests from His work creating the world. Later in the Bible, this day is called the Sabbath, and the people of Israel were to mimic God's example by resting from their work. This day of rest is mentioned multiple times throughout Exodus too.

We know from Isaiah 40:28 that God doesn't grow weary or faint, so why would He take a day to rest? I believe He rested in order to set an example for us. As mortals, we need rest. Our bodies, minds, and spirits require it, because that's how God designed us. However, the command to rest is not an excuse for laziness. God didn't intend for us to lead a life of self-indulged leisure, and the Bible contains multiple warnings to guard against laziness. But we must also be careful and guard against too much work. God intended for us to do good works, but he did not intend for us to be workaholics.

In Luke 10:38-42 we find a perfect example of the work/rest balance. In these verses we find Jesus and His disciples at the home of two sisters named Mary and Martha. Martha quickly assumes the role of hostess, busily moving about the kitchen preparing a meal for her numerous guests. Meanwhile, Mary sits at the feet of Jesus, listening to His teaching. Martha gets upset that Mary is resting instead of working, and she appeals to Jesus. But Jesus' response is not what she expected. He commended Mary for choosing to spend time resting at His feet, and He told Martha not to stress about unimportant details.

If you're like me, that story always stings a little. I am a Martha. I'm a detail-oriented planner that will sacrifice my own enjoyment to make sure everything runs smoothly for others. Consequently, I get stressed out. A good work ethic is a commendable trait, but not if it requires us to sacrifice our physical, spiritual, and mental well-being.

In Matthew 11:28 Jesus says, *"Come to me all you who are weary and burdened, and I will give you rest."* He goes on to say that if we will take up His yoke, we will find it to be easy – a light burden to bear. What does that mean? We are all guilty of placing burdens on our own backs, and we also tend to carry the burdens that people place upon us. Jesus is offering us the chance to trade those heavy burdens for His light one – one that requires us only to love God and love one another.

Bo carries no burdens. Food, water, safety and shelter are all provided for him. He can rest, because his master carries life's daily burdens for him. My Master commands me to develop a pattern of rest because it will help me stay healthy. Beyond that, He stands ready to lift all my burdens, and provide me the rest that I need.

Prayer: God, rest is part of Your original plan for mankind, so help me remember to make a place for rest in my life. When schedules are full and time is limited, teach me to rest in You. I know You stand ready to carry my burdens, so teach me to lay them down, and enter into the rest You offer.

Chapter 29: Control the Tongue

Scriptures: Matthew 12:33-37 & James 3:1-10

Key Verse: James 1:26

One of my first tasks in the morning is to let the dogs in or out the back door, depending upon where they slept that night. Taylor lies comfortably in bed, completely unaware that Scruff is preparing to spring onto the bed and lick him right across the face. It doesn't matter if he's face down or has the covers up over his head. She WILL find his face, and she WILL lick it!

Peyton is not as rambunctious in the mornings, but she too gets a little out of control with her tongue. Occasionally she feels compelled to give me a tongue bath while I'm trying to pet her. She'll lick my hand, my leg, my arm – eventually I just have to move because no matter how I try to pet her, she contorts herself into a licking position. Maybe she's trying to be sweet, but it's gross.

The tongue is such a small member of the body, and yet it does so much. It helps us talk, sing, chew, and swallow our food, and although we take it for granted, life would be challenging without it. As much as it makes our life more enjoyable, our tongues can also get us into trouble. I warn my dogs when they get a little too out of control with their tongues, and like any good master, Jesus gave us a warning when it comes to controlling our tongues.

In the middle of Matthew 12, Jesus is speaking to the religious leaders of the day. Known as the Pharisees, these men loved to concoct countless rules for the people to follow. They were sharp-tongued and judgmental, and in Matthew 12 they were at it again. Despite their religious status, in verse 34 Jesus revealed to them, and anyone else within earshot, that the words we speak are reflective of our heart – good words come from a good heart, and evil words from an evil heart. But it's verses 36 and 37 that really stand out. On judgment day everyone will give an account for the things they've said, and what we say will either leave us justified or condemned.

Jumping to the book written by Jesus' brother, the first half of James 3 contains a vivid description of the tongue and the damage it can cause. James compares it to a bit on a bridle or the rudder on a ship – such small things, and yet we can use them to turn animals of great strength and vessels of great size. So too our tongue, if we are not careful, will steer our body in a direction that will cause us great harm.

James goes on to compare the tongue to fire. When used as a tool and under control, fire is a great help and enables man accomplish much good. Unrestrained, fire can destroy vast tracts of land and everything living on that land. So it is with the tongue. It can be a tool used for building up or tearing down.

In verse eight we are told that no one can tame the tongue, but let's not forget that with God, all things are possible. If we will submit ourselves to Him and allow Him to reign over our lives, He will help us bring our tongue under control.

James 1:26 reads, *"Those who consider themselves religious and yet do not keep a tight reign on their tongues deceive themselves, and their religion is worthless."* We saw this with the Pharisees – men who claimed to be religious, but who spoke evil words from evil hearts. Religion is not what helps us control our tongues. Having a relationship with the One who rules over everything is what helps us successfully control this unruly member of our body.

Scruff and Peyton have nothing to fear when their tongues get out of control. There are no eternal ramifications for an ill-timed lick to the face. But such is not the case for me. Rather than foolishly using it to destroy others, I am expected to control my tongue, allowing God to use it for His good, and mine as well.

Prayer: God, my tongue can be used for good or evil, and I want You to use it for good. Put a guard over my mouth, and let nothing escape that is not helpful and uplifting to everyone I contact. Without Your help Lord, I cannot control this tiny member of my body, but if I will yield it to You, I know you can use it for good.

Chapter 30: Loyalty

Scriptures: Ruth 1

Key Verse: Matthew 28:20

Dogs have many wonderful traits. They are playful, protective, selfless, they never judge, but loyalty to their master might be one of their best characteristics. I think early man realized and appreciated this unique quality about their four-legged companions because throughout history, humans and dogs have always had a special connection.

Within my own pack, my dogs are unceasingly loyal to me. I can depend on them to be there when I need them, they are faithful in showing affection to me, and they are always willing to offer me protection. They cheer me up when I'm discouraged, and their constant presence brings me a sense of comfort because I know that even if the rest of the world turns against me, they will always be loyal.

We are fortunate indeed if we can find a human who can offer us this same level of loyalty. Few and far between are the friends who remain loyal through it all, and unfortunately, the same can too often be said of spouses and other family members. In our self-centered society, we care more about our own comfort and preferences, and as a result loyalty tends to fall by the wayside.

Like most things in life, loyalty is a choice. Choosing to be loyal first requires us to select to what or whom we intend to be loyal. Is it a principle, an idea, a belief that requires loyalty to survive, or is it a person, team, or organization that will receive our loyal support? What or who matters most in your life? Once you've settled that, only then can you put loyalty into action by offering your faithful support, even when it is inconvenient or comes at great cost.

The book of Ruth has only four chapters, but it contains a beautiful story about love and loyalty. Naomi and her family are Israelites who moved to the land of Moab to avoid a famine. While there, her two sons meet and marry Moabite women, one of whom is named Ruth. Tragedy strikes early on in the account, and all three women find themselves widows.

Naomi decides to return to Israel alone. She encourages her daughters-in-law to return to their families and remarry. After a tearful goodbye, one of the women agrees to Naomi's suggestion and returns to her home. Ruth, on the other hand, refuses to leave Naomi. She had come to love Naomi. She couldn't bear to let her travel the many miles back to Israel all alone, nor could she imagine the elderly widow trying to survive with no one to support her. Despite the great personal sacrifice, Ruth chose to remain with Naomi. She would leave her home, travel roads unsafe for two lone women, and work to make a home in a foreign land. Ruth knew it would not be an easy life, but she chose to remain loyal to the one she loved.

Loyalty doesn't ebb and flow as the tide, nor does it change as easily as the direction of the wind. It is constant, faithful support, regardless of the circumstances. It isn't affected by public opinion, because choosing to be loyal is a deeply personal choice. Loyalty can be one-sided, but in healthy relationships, once loyalty has been demonstrated it is then reciprocated, creating a bond between individuals that cannot be shaken.

There are many other human examples of loyalty, both biblical and modern-day, but all pale in comparison to the loyalty God displays toward us. Despite our mistakes and shortcomings, He promises to stay loyally by our side. Matthew 28:20 records Jesus' last words to His disciples as He ascended to Heaven, *"I am with you always, to the very end of the age."* God never changes, and He will always be loyal. But, as is true with our human relationships, we have to choose to be loyal to Him too.

Like my dogs, I want to be loyal to the One who cares for me. His loyalty to me led Him to the cross. His sacrifice gave me the opportunity to choose Him. I choose to lead a life that demonstrates my loyalty to the One who is with me, always.

Prayer: In this world of ever-changing loyalties, Lord, remind me that You are the only One who will never leave my side. Give me the strength and the courage to choose You over every other temptation this world as to offer. You were loyal enough to die for me, so help me be loyal enough to live for You.

Concluding Thoughts

I'd like to thank you for taking the time to walk with me through this 30-day devotional. I hope my stories brought a smile to your face. Every one of them is true and I continue to marvel at the way our Creator can use the simplest of creatures – the dog – to teach us so much about ourselves and our relationship with Him.

If you are a Christian, I hope you complete this book with a new outlook. God is near to us and makes Himself known at all times. My prayer is that you'll seek and find God in unexpected ways throughout your daily routines.

If you are not a Christian, I invite you to join me in this walk with Jesus Christ. You can become a follower of the Savior with a simple prayer like:

God, I'm a sinner who needs a Savior. I want You to be the Master of my life. I ask You to save me from my sins and the penalty that comes with them. Wash me clean and give me a fresh start. In the best way that I know how, I turn from the life I've been leading, and I commit myself to following You. I confess that You are Lord, and from this point forward, I will live and walk according to Your Word. Amen.

If you prayed that prayer, or your own version of it, let me be the first to welcome you into the flock of the Good Shepherd. Today is the first day of your journey with the One who will never leave you. We may never meet in this life, but I look forward to embracing you when we reach our eternal home.